The 25 SCARIEST HAUNTINGS in the World

Mary Batten

Illustrations by Brian Dow

Lowell House
Juvenile
Los Angeles

CONTEMPORARY BOOKS
Chicago

Publisher: Jack Artenstein
Associate Publisher, Juvenile Division: Lise Amos
Director of Publishing Services: Rena Copperman
Managing Editor, Juvenile Division: Lindsey Hay
Editor in Chief, Nonfiction: Amy Downing
Art Director: Lisa-Theresa Lenthall

Library of Congress Catalog Card Number is available

ISBN: 1-56565-486-2

Lowell House books can be purchased at special discounts when ordered in bulk for premiums and special sales. Contact Department JH at the following address:

Lowell House Juvenile
2029 Century Park East, Suite 3290
Los Angeles, CA 90067
Manufactured in the United States of America

10 9 8 7 6 5 4 3 2 1

Contents

Introduction

Mournful voices shriek in the night. A nauseating odor fills a room. An empty chair rocks back and forth . . . back and forth. Furniture breaks, lights mysteriously go on and off, and shadowy figures appear and disappear. Are these products of overactive imaginations, or is there some truth to these creepy occurrences?

Although scientists have never proved the existence of a single ghost, over the centuries people of many countries and religious faiths have believed that the dead can return to haunt the living. Every culture has its ghost stories—tales of haunted houses, castles, ships, even airplanes.

People have various explanations for ghosts: improper burial, unfinished business left by the dead, ancestors returning to protect their families, murder victims revisiting the scene of a crime, or evil persons whose spirits are doomed to the eternal punishment of having to carry out a task that will never end.

The stories in this book are the stuff of nightmares—stories that will take you into an eerie world between life and death.

Winchester Mansion: A House Built for Ghosts

Winchester Mansion, a sprawling home in San Jose, California, may be the most haunted house in the United States. Its owner, Sarah Winchester, built the home especially to please ghosts. The full story of this bizarre house didn't become public until after her death in 1922.

Sarah's home was originally in Connecticut. Her husband was William Winchester, the son and heir to the Winchester rifle fortune. In 1881 William died of tuberculosis, leaving Sarah grief-stricken and alone. Although William left Sarah $20 million, the fortune was little comfort in her grief.

Feeling quite desperate, Sarah turned to Spiritualism, a nineteenth-century movement founded on the belief that the dead communicate with the living through people known as mediums.
Sarah consulted mediums to try to contact William's spirit. Finally a Boston medium gave her a message, supposedly from William, that said: "You will be haunted forever by the ghosts of those who were killed by Winchester rifles unless you do something to make up for their untimely deaths." The medium advised her to sell all her Connecticut property, move West, and buy a house. But that wasn't all. According to the medium, as long as Sarah continued to build onto her house, the ghosts would not harm her.

SAN JOSE, CALIFORNIA

Believing that William was guiding her, in 1884 Sarah moved to California and bought an eight-room house and forty-four acres of land in San Jose, south of San Francisco. There, she believed, she would make a

home for the spirits of all those whose lives had been cut short by murder or accidents with Winchester rifles.

For thirty-eight years she kept crews of workmen busy twenty-four hours a day, seven days a week, including holidays, constructing odd-shaped rooms, stairs that ended at a ceiling, secret passageways, and doors that opened onto walls. She believed that ghosts like the number thirteen, so she had thirteen bathrooms built, with thirteen steps and thirteen windows in the thirteenth bathroom. Some of the forty staircases had thirteen steps. Many other features of the house were built in groups of thirteen. Even Sarah's will had thirteen parts, and she signed it thirteen times.

As the years of construction continued, the house grew into a rambling mansion with miles of twisting corridors and secret passageways concealed in walls.

On September 5, 1922, 83-year-old Sarah died of natural causes. By then the mansion's four stories had 160 rooms, ten thousand windows, and two thousand doors. Following Sarah's death, all building stopped, leaving certain rooms in the mansion unfinished. From that day to this, many people have reported strange events there: windows suddenly blowing open on a calm, still day; sounds of an organ such as Sarah once played; and the apparition of an old woman.

Many believe Sarah Winchester's spirit now haunts the mansion, joining the company of ghosts she spent her life trying to please.

Winchester Mystery House

On August 7, 1974, Winchester Mystery House, as Sarah Winchester's mansion is now known, was placed on the National Register of Historic Places. The house is open to the public daily except Christmas Day. Guided tours of 110 rooms depart on a regular schedule. Special tours are given every Friday the 13th and on Halloween. Prices are $12.95 for adults; $6.95 for children age 6–12; children under 5 are admitted free if accompanied by an adult. For more information, call the 24-hour information line: 408-247-2101. Or write: Winchester Mystery House, 525 South Winchester Blvd., San Jose, CA 95128.

The House of Athenodorus

In the first century A.D. the Greek philosopher Athenodorus rented an old run-down house in Athens. He would have preferred a house in better condition, but he couldn't afford it.

According to the story that was told many years later by a Roman philosopher, even before Athenodorus moved in, the house had a reputation for being haunted. People claimed they heard terrible noises at night—the clanking of chains that grew louder and louder until a phantom of a hideous old man with a long dirty beard appeared. Those who had seen him said his thin legs and wrists were fettered in chains. But Athenodorus was not afraid of ghosts; he just wanted his own place where he could read, write, and pursue his philosophical studies.

On his first night in the house, as he sat working, Athenodorus heard the clanking of chains. He was intrigued. Could there really be a ghost in the house? The sound grew louder. Suddenly the philosopher saw an old man standing before him. The ghost beckoned the philosopher with his finger, but Athenodorus refused to follow. "Go away," he muttered.

ATHENS, GREECE

The ghost shook its chains angrily until Athenodorus got up and followed. Outside in the garden the ghost pointed to a spot on the ground, then disappeared. Athenodorus marked the spot and went to bed. He did not hear any more clanking that night.

The next day Athenodorus went to the local officials and told them what had happened. A belief in ghosts was not unusual in the centuries before science, during which many people took ghosts quite seriously. The

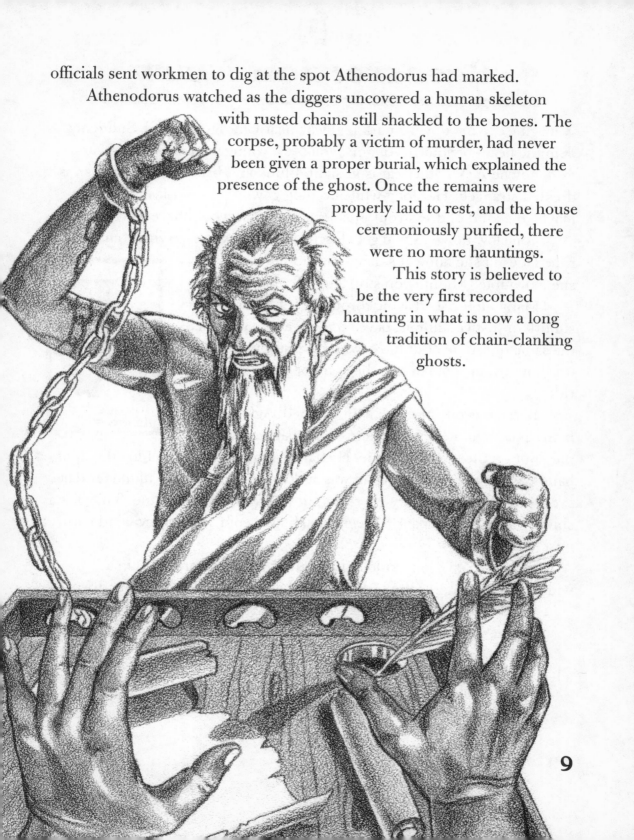

officials sent workmen to dig at the spot Athenodorus had marked. Athenodorus watched as the diggers uncovered a human skeleton with rusted chains still shackled to the bones. The corpse, probably a victim of murder, had never been given a proper burial, which explained the presence of the ghost. Once the remains were properly laid to rest, and the house ceremoniously purified, there were no more hauntings.

This story is believed to be the very first recorded haunting in what is now a long tradition of chain-clanking ghosts.

Resurrection Mary

Imagine driving down a dark highway near Chicago, Illinois. Suddenly, in the beam of your headlights, you see a young woman who appears from nowhere. No other car is in sight. Blond and beautiful, the woman is dressed strangely. Her long white evening gown looks old-fashioned, maybe the kind of dress your great-grandmother would have worn.

You slow down as you get closer to her. She waves, trying to hitch a ride. Doesn't she know it's dangerous to hitchhike? Is she in trouble? Should you stop and offer help?

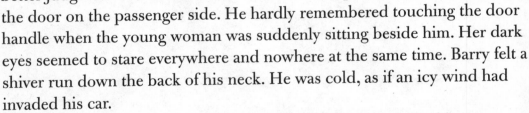

JUSTICE, ILLINOIS

Many motorists driving through the Chicago suburb of Justice, Illinois, have seen her and have asked the same questions. But those who have stopped to help this lone young woman have been in for an unforgettable ride.

Barry was one of those who stopped. Against his better judgment he reached across the seat and opened the door on the passenger side. He hardly remembered touching the door handle when the young woman was suddenly sitting beside him. Her dark eyes seemed to stare everywhere and nowhere at the same time. Barry felt a shiver run down the back of his neck. He was cold, as if an icy wind had invaded his car.

"Can you give me a ride home?" the young woman asked in a whispery voice. It was the same question she asked every obliging driver.

"And where is home?"

"Drive north on Archer Avenue," she said.

As he came to Resurrection Cemetery, she moved ever so slightly, like a leaf stirring in a breeze.

"You can let me out here," she said.

"Are you sure? There's nothing here, just a cemetery," he said uneasily.

Barry didn't remember her opening the door, but suddenly she was gone, as mysteriously as she had appeared. He strained his eyes, trying to glimpse her long white dress, but he saw only aging gray gravestones behind the cemetery fence. Only the dead resided there.

Barry is one of many unsuspecting Chicago motorists who have stopped along this dark highway to pick up the beautiful young woman known only as Resurrection Mary. Sometimes she asked for a ride to the O. Henry Ballroom, a Chicago dance hall, but the ballroom closed long ago. After that, she asked for a ride home.

Some people believe that the young woman is the ghost of a girl who was killed in an automobile accident one night in 1934 after an evening of dancing at the O. Henry Ballroom. She was buried in Resurrection Cemetery, and now she is one of Chicago's most famous ghosts.

Drivers first reported seeing Resurrection Mary around 1939. During the mid-1970s, Resurrection Cemetery was remodeled. Since then, more and more people have reported seeing the ghostly hitchhiker. Sometimes she has been seen looking through the bars of the cemetery gate. She hitches a ride at various suburban locations, but her destination is always the same—Resurrection Cemetery.

Is Resurrection Mary the ghost of a long-dead and buried young woman whose dancing ended too soon? Is she a trick of light and shadow, or a phantom of willing imaginations? If you're ever driving near Chicago at night and you see her, you'll have to decide whether you want to give this ghost a ride.

The Haunted Bridge

Anything can be haunted—a house, a ship, a battlefield, even a bridge. In Rome, Italy, the bridge known as Ponte Sisto that spans the Tiber River was said to be haunted in the seventeenth century.

On certain dark nights people walking along the bridge were startled by a sight that set them quaking, a sight they could never forget as long as they lived.

First they heard the hoofbeats of galloping horses coming closer and closer. But these were no ordinary flesh-and-blood horses. They were beasts from beyond the grave. Hardly daring to breathe, the terrified mortals watched as a black coach came into view.

Hellfires seemed to surround the coach, and the black horses raced like demons. Riding inside the blazing coach, a shriveled old woman with eyes as cold as death clutched two bags of gold.

Some people believed the old woman was the ghost of Olimpia Maidalchini Pamfili, sister-in-law of Innocent X, the Pope of the Catholic

ROME, ITALY

church from 1644–1655. When Olimpia married the Pope's elder brother, Pamfilio, she brought great wealth from her aristocratic family into the Pamfili family. At that time Innocent X, then known as Giambattista, had not become Pope. He was only a lowly cleric. From her own funds Olimpia gave him the money he needed to gain higher positions in the Catholic church. This made him feel obligated to her throughout his life. When her husband died, Olimpia, who was ambitious and domineering, took advantage of her position with Innocent X.

For many years she was considered the most powerful woman in Italy because of her influence on the Pope. Innocent X never made any important decisions without consulting her. Princes, bishops, and ambassadors sent her gifts in order to be assured they could see the Pope. Olimpia's greed was known throughout Europe, yet no one dared ignore her. Some even called her *Papessa*, which means female pope.

Gossips of the day spread that Olimpia and the Pope were more than brother- and sister-in-law—they were lovers. The Catholic church denied it, and no one believed she really loved him. She was, they said, only interested in the wealth he obtained from the church.

In those days the Catholic church controlled a great deal of money and land and was more powerful than most of Europe's governments. Popes customarily appointed members of their family to high offices in the church and loaded them with wealth and favors, sometimes to a scandalous extent. So it was that Olimpia built a great fortune at the expense of the papacy, but she was greedy for more.

According to legend, as Pope Innocent X lay dying of illness and old age, Olimpia sat beside his bed, waiting for him to take his last breath. As soon as he died, she stole two boxes of gold from under his bed. She told no one that he was dying and offered him no comfort in his final hours. She wouldn't even pay for a wooden casket for his burial, claiming she was a poor widow.

After Olimpia died, the ghostly coach with its phantom rider and demon horses began to appear on the Ponte Sisto bridge. People believed that the fiery coach ride was Olimpia's punishment for the cold, hurtful way she had treated her brother-in-law. "When the coach stops," they said, "Donna Olimpia will be in hell."

No one ever saw the coach stop. It always crossed the bridge, went down the bank, and disappeared into the river.

Stealing from the Dead: The Squire of Swinsty Hall

By a stream in Hampshire, England, a shriveled old man known only as Robinson scrubs and rinses a pile of coins. He has been at his task for centuries, and he will never finish, for he is a ghost serving eternal punishment for the foul deeds he committed in life.

Like a vulture, Robinson preyed on the dead. Bodies were hardly cold when he crept into houses, stealing whatever valuables he could find. His

HAMPSHIRE, ENGLAND

greed was so great that he even stole coins that had been placed on the eyes of corpses to keep their souls from escaping. To Robinson, death was an opportunity, for after all, the dead had no use for money and jewels.

And in London in 1665 there was a lot of death. The streets stank with the odor of bodies, victims of the most horrible epidemic that ever swept medieval Europe—the bubonic plague. At that time people did not know that bubonic plague germs were carried by tiny fleas that lived on rats—rats that were everywhere, in every crack and crevice of old London.

In the midst of this horror Robinson carried on his evil trade, and somehow he managed to avoid catching the plague himself. Then, a year later, London caught on fire. The Great Fire of 1666 destroyed most of the city, but it also ended the plague by incinerating the fleas that carried the plague germs.

As the flames swept through the city, many Londoners, including Robinson, fled for their lives. Carrying his ill-gotten fortune, Robinson moved to the village where he was born. But he was not welcomed. The villagers feared he would contaminate them with the dreaded plague, and they drove him away.

For a while he lived in an old barn on the outskirts of the village and tried to clean his stolen coins by washing them in a stream. Eventually he moved to Hampshire, England, and used his money to build a fine mansion that he called Swinsty Hall. There he lived in luxury until he died, but death was not to be his final resting place.

For many years after Robinson's death people reported seeing a hunched-over little old man endlessly scrubbing a pile of coins in a stream not far from Swinsty Hall. According to local stories, this was his punishment for eternity. Never to find peace, Robinson's ghost may still be washing his filthy money.

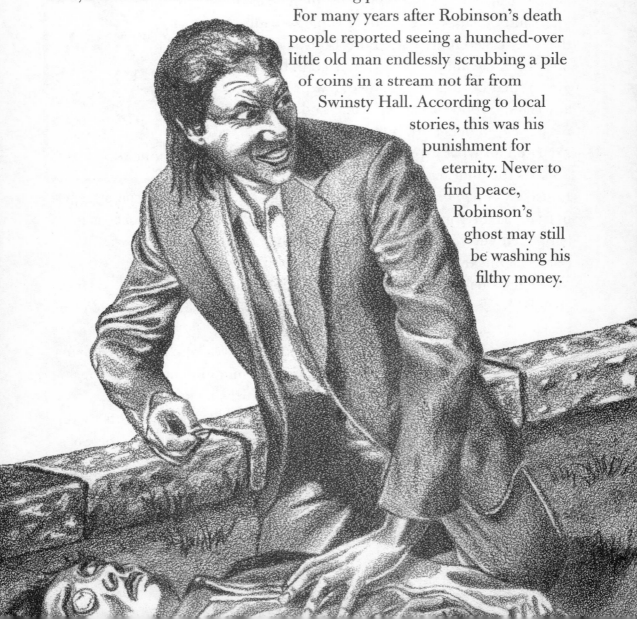

Bad Lord Lonsdale

Some ghosts are kindly, protective spirits; others are angry, returning to make life as miserable as possible for the family members who survive them. Lord Lonsdale's ghost was one of the angriest ever known.

Even when he was alive in the late 1780s, Lord Lonsdale was a mean man. He argued with his neighbors. He beat the peasants who worked his land, because they couldn't pay his high taxes of grain and livestock. He treated people so badly that they called him "Bad" Lord Lonsdale. No one ever knew him to do a kind deed in his life.

When Lord Lonsdale died, few people shed any tears. "Good riddance," some said. "May he rot in hell," others said. But nobody was prepared for what happened at the funeral.

WESTMORLAND, ENGLAND

As the minister prayed over Lord Lonsdale's open coffin, the corpse suddenly sat up. The mourners gasped in fright as the corpse's eyes opened and bulged. Then, as quickly as it happened, the corpse's eyes closed and the body lay back on its satin pillows. Quickly the minister closed the coffin.

Everyone was relieved to get Lord Lonsdale's body into the ground, covered by six feet of dirt. Little did they know that they had not seen—or heard—the last of him.

Soon after Lord Lonsdale's burial, the relatives who continued living in his home, Lowther Hall, reported a great commotion on the upper floors. Night after night they heard the Bad Lord's bellowing voice, shouting angrily as he had done so many times in life. Other nights there were loud crashes as if someone were throwing furniture against the walls or smashing chairs on the floor.

When the house grew quiet again, they would tiptoe cautiously into the hallway. Then the ghost would sometimes appear at the top of the great staircase and glower menacingly at those cringing below. There was no peace in Lowther Hall.

Nor was there much peace outside the house. Some nights neighbors said they saw Bad Lord Lonsdale's ghost driving a ghostly black coach and whipping the phantom horses into a panic. When they saw the coach, people feared for their lives and tried to get their carriages off the road. Terrified, some lost control and drove into a ditch.

For years Bad Lord Lonsdale's ghost terrorized people throughout Westmorland. Everybody wanted his ghost to return to its grave and stay there, but no amount of prayer or lucky charms seemed to work.

The terror continued for several months. Finally, a neighbor who was wise in the art of quieting angry spirits, used his skill against the ghost. No one knows exactly what he did. He may have scattered cloves of garlic throughout the house, or he may have frightened the ghost by reading from the Bible. Whatever he did, Lowther Hall and the countryside of Westmorland became peaceful. After the end of the nineteenth century, the ghost of Bad Lord Lonsdale was seen no more.

The Ghosts of Versailles

VERSAILLES, FRANCE

One hot August morning around the turn of the twentieth century, Anne Moberly and Eleanor Jourdain arrived at Versailles, the elegant seventeenth century country home built by the French king Louis XIV. The women were excited about touring the palace that no one had lived in for more than a century. Or so the two women thought.

After visiting the grand palace, Ms. Moberly and Ms. Jourdain decided to walk to the Petit Trianon, one of several smaller palaces built at Versailles by Louis XIV's descendants.

As they walked through a woods and into a clearing, Ms. Moberly saw a woman shaking out a white cloth. Ms. Jourdain did not see the woman. Suddenly both Ms. Moberly and Ms. Jourdain felt an intense and strange sadness that neither could explain.

Then they met two gardeners dressed in green and wearing unusual three-cornered hats. "Which way to the Petit Trianon?" asked Ms. Jourdain in French.

One of the men pointed silently with his spade, and the two women continued walking, but soon they felt hopelessly lost.

Then they heard footsteps running behind them, and a young man, wearing eighteenth century clothes and buckled shoes, appeared. Pointing to the right, he told them in French, "Go this way to find the house."

Ms. Moberly and Ms. Jourdain followed the mysterious man's advice and turned right, crossing a bridge over a ravine with a small waterfall. They found themselves in a garden leading to a château—the Petit Trianon.

On the terrace Ms. Moberly saw a woman wearing a long white dress decorated with a pale green triangular scarf called a fichu. She was sketching but looked up as they passed. Ms. Jourdain didn't see anything and thought the house was deserted. Again, both women felt an overwhelming sense of sadness and depression.

Soon another young man appeared and led them through the house and out the front door. A wedding was going on, but nobody paid any attention to the English tourists. As soon as Ms. Moberly and Ms. Jourdain left, their feelings of sadness and depression vanished.

When they returned to their hotel, they were too tired to talk about what they had seen, but they wrote in their diaries. Later when they compared notes, they concluded they must have seen ghosts.

Ms. Moberly and Ms. Jourdain returned to Versailles to look for the bridge, the waterfall, and the people they had seen before, but all had disappeared. They discovered the door their guide had led them through had been blocked for a century, and gardeners last wore the green uniforms and hats in 1789. All had been ghostly images.

Further research revealed that on August 10, 1792, three days after Queen Marie Antoinette and other royal family members had been in the garden at the Petit Trianon, they were in Paris, fleeing angry mobs.

The two women were struck by the date. It was on August 10 that they had first visited Versailles and seen the ghosts. They theorized that perhaps on that very date, more than a century earlier, Queen Marie Antoinette realized all was lost and tried to hold in her mind the images of her last moments of pleasure. Perhaps those feelings were so intense they made an imprint on the house, a kind of ghostly video recording that is replayed year after year, haunting those who chance to visit on a certain day in August.

The Ghosts of Yotsuya

Many years ago in Yotsuya, an area of central Tokyo, there lived a samurai, or warrior, named Iyemon (E-yeh-mon). He was married to a beautiful woman named Oiwa (O-E-wah), and they had a baby boy whom they adored. Unable to find a job as a samurai, he became an umbrella maker.

As Iyemon went about his work, he would occasionally see his neighbor's daughter Oume (O-oo-meh). Despite his own wife, Iyemon was attracted to Oume, and she was also drawn to him.

One day Iyemon asked Oume's father, a doctor, for some medicine for Oiwa, who was weak from childbirth. Perhaps the doctor misunderstood what Iyemon wanted; or perhaps, because he knew his own daughter's feelings, he had his own evil intentions. In any case, the medicine was a poison that transformed Oiwa into a monstrous-looking woman.

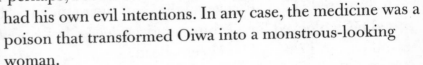

TOKYO, JAPAN

Oiwa was horrified by what had happened to her face, but she was even more devastated by her husband's reaction. Instead of comfort, Iyemon felt only disgust. He began to abuse Oiwa, hoping to drive her away.

Oiwa became so depressed with her looks and Iyemon's abuse that she killed herself and their son. When Iyemon returned home and discovered the tragedy, Oiwa's servant Kohei (ko-hay) confronted him: "It's your fault. You drove her to this with your cruelty." Iyemon was already angry that Oiwa had killed their son, but he became more enraged that a servant would dare scold him. Drawing his sword, he murdered Kohei. Then he nailed Oiwa's and Kohei's bodies to a plank and threw them into a river.

Iyemon was now free to marry Oume, and preparations were made for the wedding. Oume wore the bride's traditional white hood that covers the face. After the ceremony, Iyemon lifted Oume's hood and was horrified to see what he thought was Oiwa's hideously deformed face. But Oiwa was dead! He drew his sword and ran it through his new bride. At once Iyemon realized that instead of killing Oiwa's ghost, he had killed Oume.

Hysterical with fright, Iyemon ran to the river where he had dumped the bodies of Oiwa and Kohei. In a daze, he thought he saw the plank with the two bodies floating by. He imagined the two ghosts crying out to him. Iyemon threw himself into the river and drowned.

Oiwa's grave still exists in Aoyama (Ah-O-yah-mah) Cemetery in Tokyo. Her story was dramatized as a Kabuki play, and films have been made about her. Before filming, the filmmakers go to Oiwa's grave and ask her spirit not to harm the actors or crew. But there's no need; Oiwa's ghost has already had its revenge. The ghost only haunted the evil Iyemon and was never seen again after his death.

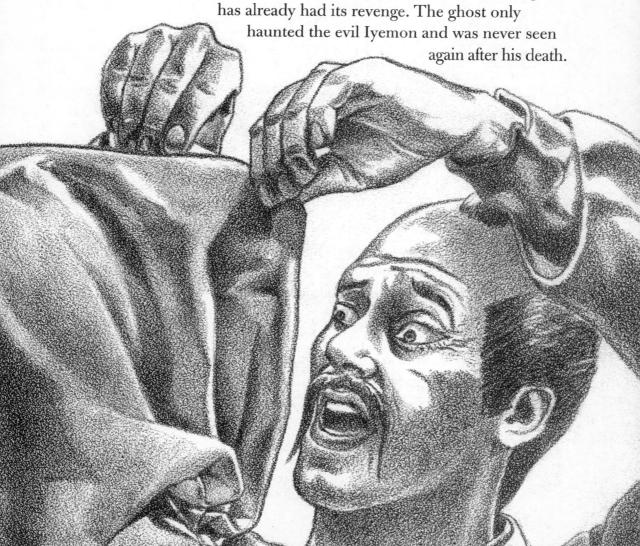

Ghosts in the White House

Not even presidents, queens, and prime ministers are immune to ghosts. Many a famous visitor, as well as famous residents of the White House, has reported seeing or feeling strange presences, most especially the ghost of Abraham Lincoln, the sixteenth president of the United States.

During the spring of 1865, President Lincoln began having premonitions of his death. Ten days before his actual assassination, Lincoln dreamed that he would be killed. He confided his chilling dream to Mrs. Lincoln and Ward H. Lamon, one of his most trusted bodyguards, who often warned Lincoln about his safety.

WASHINGTON, D.C.

For three nights Lincoln dreamed he would be killed. On April 14, 1865, he confided the disturbing dreams to another bodyguard, William H. Crook. Crook knew that the Lincolns planned on attending the theater that very evening. Lincoln told Crook that if he hadn't made a commitment to go, he would remain at the White House. But he felt that he could not disappoint the people.

It was at Ford's Theater in Washington, D.C., on that fateful evening, that Lincoln was assassinated by actor John Wilkes Booth, who violently opposed the president's antislavery policy. The murder has never been forgotten, especially by those who claim they have seen Lincoln's ghost.

The first person to see Lincoln's ghost in the White House was Grace Coolidge, wife of President Calvin Coolidge, who served from 1923 to 1929. More than fifty-eight years after Lincoln's death, she reportedly saw his silhouette standing at a window in the Oval Office. Twentieth-century

writer Carl Sandburg, who won a Pulitzer Prize for his six-volume biography of Lincoln, once said he felt, but did not see, Lincoln standing by him at the same window. Sandburg made many visits to the White House while he was researching the biography.

Although more than a century has passed since Lincoln was murdered, some people continue to report seeing his ghost or hearing strange sounds in the White House, especially in Lincoln's bedroom, which is now called the Lincoln Room.

Dutch Queen Wilhelmina once visited President Franklin D. Roosevelt and told him of hearing footsteps in the corridor outside the Lincoln Room, where she was spending the night. Upon hearing a knock at the door, she opened it and saw Lincoln standing before her.

25

The queen fainted. Winston Churchill, the British Prime Minister, believed he saw Lincoln's ghost. Eleanor Roosevelt, wife of President Roosevelt, often sensed Lincoln's presence, usually late at night when she was writing at her desk. President Harry Truman also believed he heard Lincoln walking about.

As recently as 1987, *The Wall Street Journal* reported that Maureen Reagan, daughter of President Ronald Reagan, and her husband, Dennis Revell, allegedly saw Lincoln's ghost in the Lincoln Room, which they often occupied. Maureen Reagan described the ghost as "a transparent person."

Although Lincoln is the White House's most famous ghost, there are others. The ghosts of First Ladies Dolley Madison and Abigail Adams are also said to haunt the presidential home. If the legend can be believed, Dolley Madison's ghost was angry when Mrs. Woodrow Wilson wanted to dig up her rose garden. The garden won out and is still there.

Although the White House is the home of the current, living president and his family, some of its past residents may never have left.

The Weird Weirs of Bow Head

Nobody suspected there was anything weird about Major Thomas Weir, a highly respected citizen of Edinburgh in the seventeenth century. Major Weir and his sister, Jean, lived at Bow Head, the family home. They were quiet, decent people and well liked by their neighbors. They never caused trouble for anyone. So the townspeople were stunned by the major's confession of deeds so foul that only a demon could have committed them.

When Major Weir was seventy years old, he announced that he practiced witchcraft and black magic, and that he had abused young girls.

The townspeople were shocked and terrified. They felt tricked by the Weirs, whom they had treated with respect. They were at a loss to understand how such people, living in their midst, could be so evil. "They must be punished," people said. "Make them pay. Make them pay."

EDINBURGH, SCOTLAND

On April 29, 1670, the Weirs were tried for their crimes. Doctors and clergymen tried to help Weir, but he cursed them. "I find nothing within me but blackness and darkness, brimstone and burning to the bottom of hell," he said.

Both Weirs were found guilty and sentenced to death. On April 11, 1670, Major Weir was strangled at a stake and then burned. The next day Jean was hanged.

After the executions, the citizens of Edinburgh tried to return to their normal lives. But this was not to be. People began seeing and hearing strange things at the Weirs' home. A phantom coach was said to arrive at

the door to take Weir and his sister away to hell. Some people reported seeing a ghost wearing a cloak and clutching Weir's staff, which was believed to possess magical powers.

For almost a century Bow Head remained unoccupied. Without care, the old house deteriorated, and the landlord drastically reduced the rent to attract a tenant. A poor elderly couple moved in. On their first night in the house they reported seeing a calf staring at them through the window. Being superstitious, the couple interpreted the calf as an evil sign, and they moved out the next day. No one else ever lived in the home.

But the hauntings did not stop. In 1825 people reported seeing lights and hearing sounds of dancing and howling in the house. Weir's magical staff was said to march—on its own—through the house. Some said they saw the major's ghost riding a headless black horse galloping out of an alley at midnight. The horse, they said, was surrounded by a whirlwind of flames.

By 1830 the house was in ruins, so it was demolished. Still, some people said they heard Weir's old staff rapping on the ground and saw his sister's face hovering over the site where the house once stood.

The Ghosts of Flight 401

On the evening of December 29, 1972, Eastern Flight 401 radioed the control tower at Miami that it was making its landing approach. The flight had been perfect. Captain Bob Loft and second officer Dan Repo were guiding the big plane's descent. That's when the pilots discovered a problem with the landing gear warning light. It seemed a minor problem. It just meant circling again to make a second landing approach. All fairly routine, or so the pilots believed.

As they focused on solving the problem, they didn't realize that the plane had been steadily losing altitude. When they finally noticed how much altitude had been lost, it was too late to make a correction. The plane crashed into the dark Everglades, killing the crew and 100 passengers.

When rescuers arrived, bodies were strewn everywhere. Captain Loft survived for about an hour after the crash but died in the cockpit. Repo was alive when rescuers pulled him from the wreckage, but he died in the hospital about thirty hours after the crash.

FLORIDA
EVERGLADES

To save money, Eastern officials decided to salvage whatever parts they could from the wreckage and use them in other Eastern planes. It was then that many Eastern crew members began having experiences that sent chills up their spines.

For almost two years pilots and flight attendants reported seeing ghosts of Loft, Repo, and some unidentified flight attendants from Flight 401 on various other Eastern flights. The ghosts were seen most often on planes containing parts from the plane that had crashed, but they were sighted on other planes as well.

Several times Captain Loft's ghost was seen sitting in a plane's first-class section. On one of these occasions a flight attendant asked Loft why his name was not on her passenger list. There was only silence. The attendant went to her captain for advice. When he looked into the cabin, the captain instantly recognized Loft. At that moment the ghost disappeared.

On other occasions Loft's ghost appeared in the crew compartment. Once Loft's voice made an announcement to passengers about seat belts and smoking rules.

Repo's ghost was seen even more often than Loft's. Crew members who saw Repo said that his ghost was especially concerned about safety. Sometimes Repo's ghost was seen in the cockpit checking instruments. Once Repo's ghost told an engineer that he had already made the preflight inspection. On other occasions, he pointed out a problem in the plane's hydraulic system and warned an attendant about a fire on the plane.

Eastern employees who saw the ghosts were afraid to talk about them. Some who did were advised to see a psychiatrist, and they feared they would lose their jobs.

Reports of the ghosts were so widespread that Eastern finally removed all the airplane parts salvaged from the ill-fated Flight 401. But they can't get rid of the memories the ghosts left behind, for no one who saw any of the ghostly crew will ever forget.

La Llorona: the Weeping Woman of Mexico

Dressed in a long flowing black or white dress, she is seen walking alongside rivers or on lonely roads in Mexico. Tears continually stream down her face. Who is she?

Many Mexicans and Mexican-Americans call her La Llorona, Spanish for "weeper." They believe La Llorona is the ghost of an Indian princess, Doña Luis de Olveros, who lived in Mexico City around 1550. According to legend, the princess fell in love with a wealthy nobleman and bore him two children. Although he promised to marry her, he married someone else instead. When Doña Luis found out, she became hysterical with anger and humiliated at his treachery. With a dagger he had given her as a gift, she stabbed their children to death. Then she wandered the streets, crying desperately for her children. She was arrested, found guilty, and hanged. Her ghost is believed to be cursed to wander the earth forever, searching for the children she murdered.

MEXICO

Since the sixteenth century La Llorona has been seen throughout Mexico and even in parts of the American Southwest. There are different versions of the story and different descriptions of the ghost. Some say she has long black hair and long clawlike fingernails. In some accounts she is faceless; in others she has the face of a bat, a horse, or a vampire.

Like the ghosts in many other hauntings, La Llorona seems sentenced

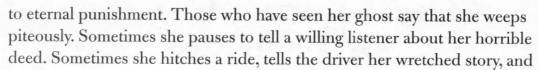

to eternal punishment. Those who have seen her ghost say that she weeps piteously. Sometimes she pauses to tell a willing listener about her horrible deed. Sometimes she hitches a ride, tells the driver her wretched story, and then disappears. Over and over she relives the chilling details of her children's murders.

Some people believe that anyone who sees La Llorona will die or have bad luck within a year. Some believe she preys on young men who have had too much to drink. Whatever you believe, hope that you never see La Llorona on a lonely Mexican road at night.

33

The Moving Coffins of Barbados

When the Chase family crypt was unsealed for a family burial in July 1819, the mourners were in for a shock. The heavy lead coffins inside the crypt looked as if they had been tossed around like toy blocks.

The local people were scared. They believed that some evil spirit was afoot, for this was not the first time that coffins in the Chase tomb had moved.

CHRIST CHURCH, BARBADOS

Lord Combermere, the English governor of the island of Barbados, wanted to quiet people's fears by proving that no one could break into the crypt and move the coffins. After the funeral, he left his own seal in the mortar used to close the door to the tomb.

Nine months later, on April 18, 1820, he ordered the tomb reopened. Hundreds of islanders gathered to witness the event. Lord Combermere felt reassured to see that his seal had not been broken. It took several large men to move the heavy stone slab that sealed the vault. When the slab was finally moved enough so that people could look inside, they shuddered and gasped at the sight. The governor, too, was shocked. Once again the coffins had been moved. One of the tiny coffins that contained a baby had a deep gash as if it had been thrown against the stone wall. How could such a thing have happened? People were sure it was the work of ghosts; some even thought they knew why.

Colonel Thomas Chase, a wealthy Englishman who lived in Christ Church, Barbados, bought the crypt early in the nineteenth century. Local people never liked Chase. They said he was cruel and short-tempered.

The first family member was laid to rest in the tomb in the summer of 1807. The lead coffin was so heavy it took four men to lift it. A few months later Chase's infant daughter was buried in the crypt. These two coffins were in their original positions when the tomb was opened on July 6, 1812, for the burial of Dorcas Chase, another of the colonel's daughters. Some people said Dorcas starved herself to death because Chase had treated her so cruelly.

The next month, August 1812, Chase himself died. The rumor was that Chase had been so grief-stricken by Dorcas's death that he committed suicide. When the vault was opened for Chase's burial, the other three coffins had mysteriously moved. Some people thought that vandals had broken into the tomb and moved the coffins. But others suspected ghosts.

Workmen returned the coffins to their original positions side by side and placed Chase's coffin on top and across them. To detect vandalism, a layer of sand was spread on the floor.

The crypt wasn't opened again until four years later, in 1816. Once again the coffins were found scattered around the crypt, but the sand was not disturbed. This seemed to rule out vandals who would have left footprints in the sand.

The coffins were rearranged side by side and another layer of sand spread around them. When a family member was buried in the tomb a few weeks later, the coffins had moved. Once again the sand was not disturbed.

The islanders began talking about "duppies," as they called evil spirits. They felt that the moving coffins were a sign that other family members buried before Colonel Chase didn't want his body in the crypt with theirs.

In 1820, after Governor Combermere failed to dispel fears about evil spirits, the remaining members of the Chase family moved all the coffins to another burial place. The vault was then permanently sealed, never to be used again.

The One-Armed Ghost of Castello di Bracciano

BRACCIANO, ITALY

It is always in the dead of night when the clanking of metal is heard, echoing through the stone hallways of the great medieval castle of Bracciano. The sounds grow louder and a door opens. A young man wearing armor enters. He is wet, with seaweed tangled in his hair and lake slime on his rusted armor. His right arm is missing. Sometimes the figure moans as if in pain. Then he disappears, leaving a trail of muddy water. It is the ghost of Attilio Orsini.

Attilio was the favorite son of Guidobaldo Orsini, a warrior so fierce and cunning he was called Lupo Vecchio, which means the Old Wolf. Throughout the 1400s the powerful Orsini and Colonna families were at war with each other, and victory passed back and forth between the two houses. Although Guidobaldo's forces had won the latest battle, it was at great cost. His two sons, Attilio and Danielo, had been killed. Guidobaldo's only remaining male descendant was his grandson, Attilio's young son, Arco. But Arco, crippled by rickets, could hardly walk. He spent his days lying on fox-fur cushions near his grandfather.

Guidobaldo wanted more than anything to avenge Attilio's death. But when he learned that the Colonnas planned to storm the castle, he worried. The castle had withstood the Colonnas' attacks before, but this time Guidobaldo knew that he was old and too sick to fight. With his grandson an invalid, there was no Orsini in Bracciano to lead the attack.

That night in his bedchamber Guidobaldo heard the familiar clanking noise. He was not afraid, for Attilio's ghost had visited the old man many

37

times. Each time the ghost went to the table where Guidobaldo kept the piece of armor that had covered his son's right arm, the one that Roderigo Colonna had hacked off and thrown into Lake Bracciano alongside Attilio's body. On this night Attilio's ghost pointed to the family banner and then to the fox-fur cushions. Guidobaldo realized his son's ghost was telling him that Arco must lead the Orsinis into battle with the Colonnas. But how? The boy could hardly stand. Before Guidobaldo could talk to the ghost, it disappeared.

The next morning Guidobaldo received heartbreaking news. Little Arco had died during the night.

The Colonna troops were now stationed around the castle, readying their attack. Then luck intervened for Guidobaldo. It began to rain. The lake waters rose, drowning many Colonna soldiers.

After four days the weather cleared, and Guidobaldo ordered that the body of his grandson be strapped in the finest suit of armor.

At first light the Orsini men-at-arms, riding in a protective wedge around their small, stiff leader, charged the mud-soaked Colonna troops. Old Roderigo Colonna, murderer of Arco's father, rode to meet the new Orsini leader. Immediately the Orsini men-at-arms struck down the elder Colonna. The battle was over. Although he would never know it, Arco had led his family to victory and avenged his father's murder.

With great ceremony Arco was buried in the family crypt. That night, while praying at the altar in the crypt, Guidobaldo died, his sword in his hands. But this was not the end of the Orsini family.

In the five centuries since Guidobaldo's death, ghosts have continued to haunt the old castle. Local villagers have seen Attilio's one-armed ghost walking near Lake Bracciano. Sometimes he crosses the meadow and enters the room that had been Guidobaldo's bedchamber. Even the ghost of the Old Wolf, Guidobaldo, has been seen kneeling in the crypt. Although Bracciano Castle has been owned by the wealthy Odescalchi family since 1696, at least two ghostly members of the Orsini family are still there.

The Haunting of the Smurls

WEST PITTSTON, PENNSYLVANIA

It seemed like a nice house in a good neighborhood when John and Mary Smurl, their son, Jack, and his wife, Janet, bought it in 1973. The house, built in 1896, needed a lot of work, but the Smurls enjoyed remodeling. In 1974 the two families, which included Jack and Janet's adolescent daughters, Dawn and Heather, were just beginning to feel comfortable in their new home when mysterious things began to happen.

They heard footsteps on the stairs but found no one. Dawn said she saw people floating around her bedroom. Toilets flushed on their own. Unplugged radios blared. Empty porch chairs rocked. Strange smells filled the house. By 1977 the Smurls suspected their house must be haunted. In that same year Janet gave birth to twin daughters, Shannon and Carin.

The hauntings continued to disturb the family over the next eight years, but in 1985 they became frightening. In February Janet saw a tall, faceless human shape in her kitchen. A ceiling light crashed down on Shannon, then eight years old, nearly killing her. In June something pulled Janet off her bed. Phantom dogs were seen running through the house. Neighbors heard screams and strange noises coming from the house when the Smurls weren't there.

Terrified, but refusing to be driven from their home by ghosts, in 1986 the Smurls called in psychic researchers Ed and Lorraine Warren. After investigating the house, the Warrens said they detected four evil spirits. Three were minor, but the fourth was a demon. The Warrens theorized that the demon may have been quiet for years but must have been aroused by the energy coming from the twin girls, who were entering puberty.

The researchers played religious music and prayed, trying to get the demon to reveal itself. Janet even tried to talk to the demon. "Rap once for yes and twice for no," she said. Then she asked, "Are you here to harm us?" The response was ominous: one rap.

See It on Film
A movie version of the Smurls' story, called *The Haunted*, was released in 1991. Check it out at your local video store. It stars Sally Kirkland.

The Warrens brought in a Catholic priest who performed an exorcism—a ceremony to get rid of evil spirits. But the attacks only increased. A second exorcism also failed, and the demon then began to haunt the family away from the house, such as on camping trips.

By this time the Smurl house hauntings were getting publicity, and the family agreed to be interviewed on a local television talk show, so long as their faces weren't seen. After the show Jack said he saw the demon—a pig-like animal on two legs.

In September 1986 the priest performed a third exorcism, which seemed to work. But within three months Jack saw the menacing form again. Unable to remain in the house any longer, they moved to another town in 1988, just before their book about their experience, *The Haunted*, was published. The Catholic church performed a fourth exorcism in 1989. This seemed to bring peace to the family at last.

The Ghostrider of Labrador

Esau Gillingham was a fur trapper who moved from Newfoundland to Labrador around the early part of the twentieth century. Trapping was hard work, and it was difficult to make a living.

Esau saw a way to make some easy money with "moonshine," or homemade liquor. During the frozen winter months people used rum as medicine and to warm their bodies, but it was scarce. So, Esau set up a secret still—an apparatus for making alcoholic liquor—and made moonshine from spruce cones, sugar, and yeast. The Labrador trappers called the brew "smoke," and gave Esau the nickname "Smoker." His moonshine had the reputation for making people crazy. In fact, some fell over dead-drunk in the snow and froze to death after drinking it.

LABRADOR, CANADA

Making moonshine was illegal, and the police arrested Smoker and put him in jail for a year. When he got out, he swore he'd never be inside again.

Smoker devised a plan to hide from the police. He began trapping only animals with white skins. When he had enough skins, he made himself a white fur suit. He stole every white husky he could find, built a white sled, and then lashed a white keg to it. Now Smoker blended in so well with the snow-covered environment that he seemed invisible. He started his deadly business again.

Smoker sold his illegal liquor for years. The police tried to capture him, but they couldn't find him. Then, through an informer, a person paid to give the police information, they arrested Smoker in 1934. They threatened to lock him up if he didn't lead them to the still.

Smoker led the police to the site of the still but then warned them that the area was protected by bear traps that could break a man's leg. Not wanting to risk injury, the police decided not to walk into the area. Since they didn't actually see the still, the police had no evidence. They released Smoker and never caught him again.

Smoker returned to Newfoundland and, in 1940, fell off a platform where fish were dried near the Gander River. He broke his back and died three days later in great pain. As he lay dying, Smoker was terrified of going to hell and he prayed, "Oh, God, please don't send me to hell! Just let me drive my dogs along the coast to the end of time. I'll make up for all the bad things I've done."

To this day local people who have seen Smoker's ghost say that he meets lost teams and guides them home in storms. They can almost always tell when the ghostly team is coming, because dogs howl and the weather turns especially nasty.

The Jeweled Skeleton of Inés de Castro

For centuries people in Braga, Portugal, have seen the ghost of the beautiful young woman with long golden hair who haunts the countryside. In life she was Inés de Castro, wife of Dom Pedro, heir to the Portuguese throne in the mid-1300s. She was known throughout Portugal for her beauty, but she was a commoner; and Dom Pedro's father, King Alfonso, opposed the marriage, as did many of the loyal aristocrats, or nobles, in his court. King Alfonso wanted his son to marry an heiress of noble birth who would add her family's wealth to Dom Pedro's.

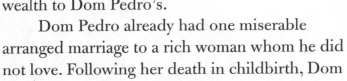

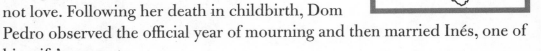

BRAGA, PORTUGAL

Dom Pedro already had one miserable arranged marriage to a rich woman whom he did not love. Following her death in childbirth, Dom Pedro observed the official year of mourning and then married Inés, one of his wife's servants.

For several years they were very happy, and they had three children. But the feelings of his father, Alfonso, and the nobles did not change. The thought of Inés becoming queen of Portugal one day only increased their hatred of her.

Dom Pedro looked forward to becoming king and making Inés his queen. In his eagerness he made a most unfortunate decision. He hired an artist to paint Inés's portrait wearing the crown jewels and coronation robes. Had he hidden the painting until he became king, the sad events to come might have been avoided. But Dom Pedro wanted to show off the painting, and he unveiled it at a banquet. For the nobles, this queenly painting of a woman they hated was too much. With King Alfonso's approval, they began to plot Inés's destruction.

The treacherous deed was set for the day of Dom Pedro's great hunt. Everyone except the servants, Inés, and her three small children would leave the hunting lodge at dawn. Dom Pedro's two sons from his first marriage were old enough to go along on the hunt.

Soon after the hunting party left that fateful morning, Inés heard her servants screaming. Trying to reach her children, she raced upstairs, but she was not fast enough. Rough hands grabbed her. Her three children ran to her side only to be slaughtered one by one. The last thing Inés saw was her assassin's sword aimed at her own heart.

When Dom Pedro returned and discovered the horror, he threw himself on the floor beside Inés's body and would not move. His loyal guards took him to his bedchamber, where he lay for months, hardly eating or speaking.

Finally realizing that he must carry on with his life, he moved to Lisbon and prepared for the day he would become king. Not long thereafter Alfonso died and Dom Pedro was crowned King Pedro I of Portugal in 1357. His first act was to arrest the three traitors who had killed his wife and children. Certain nobles were only too willing to identify the assassins in hopes of gaining favor with King Pedro. He had the murderers tortured and ordered their hearts ripped from their bodies. Then, according to legend, he prepared the strangest coronation ever known.

He commanded all the nobles to attend the ceremony. None dared disobey, for they knew what had happened to the traitors. In the glow of hundreds of candles, the trembling nobles and their wives approached the throne. Seated beside the king was the skeleton of Inés de Castro, dressed in velvet robes. Around her bony neck and fingers were the royal jewels.

Fearing for their lives, the nobles bowed before their grotesque queen and kissed the hem of her coronation robe. The jeweled corpse of Inés de Castro had reigned as Queen of Portugal . . . at least for one day.

Since that time many have reported seeing a wounded woman frantically running back and forth along the balcony of the hunting lodge where Inés was murdered. Sometimes she runs from the gates and crosses the road. Other times she has been seen walking in the private chapel of the palace of the kings of Portugal at Oporto.

The Bloody Ghost of St. Bavon

GHENT, BELGIUM

The story of the bloody ghost begins in the 1300s, when Count Alard lived in the castle of Bavon with his second wife and their two sons. Also living in the castle were three other sons from his first marriage to Countess Ygraine d'Oultremont-Mérode. Countess Ygraine had been poisoned by a treacherous man pretending to be a friend, and Count Alard had never fully recovered from her murder.

Among the count's many servants was his children's trusted nurse, Blanfar, who had worked for the count since his first son was born.

After the count's second marriage, Blanfar brought her teenage son, Nold, to the castle. She begged Count Alard to give the boy work so they could be near each other. The count hired Nold as an assistant to his armorer.

Count Alard changed drastically after the murder of his first wife. He never joked or laughed. He drank too much, carried a whip, and often struck men in the face if they angered him.

The new countess tried to please him, but nothing she did made him happy. Blanfar noticed the change, as did everyone else.

Blanfar blamed the count's personality change on the new countess, whom she began to dislike. Blanfar's distaste for the countess grew, as the countess became very critical of Nold. On one occasion the countess discovered Nold flirting with one of her serving maids. She scolded the boy, told him he could not leave the armory, and informed Count Alard. The count warned Nold never to speak to his wife's maids again.

One night Count Alard got very drunk. Taking his whip and wearing full battle armor, he walked through the corridors of his castle. By chance he came upon Nold with the same serving maid. The count became enraged. Out of control, he hit Nold repeatedly with the heavy iron handle of the whip and left him bleeding on the cold stone floor.

The maid ran to Blanfar. Before morning, Nold died in his mother's arms. Grief-stricken, Blanfar was determined to get revenge. Quietly she made her plans.

Over the next year, while Count Alard was away at war, tragedy struck his sons. Three died of mysterious accidents. Blanfar usually discovered each body, but the count never suspected her because of her trusted position.

Only Ygnall, the first-born son, and Ligne, the third-born, were left. The count summoned Ygnall, now a grown man, to join him in battle.

Before Ygnall left, he asked for a bowl of hot soup. Blanfar brought him one of her homemade broths. During his journey to meet his father Ygnall fell ill and died of poisoning.

When word of Ygnall's death reached the count, he realized Blanfar must have poisoned him. Immediately he suspected she was also responsible for the deaths of his other sons. Fearing for Ligne's life, Count Alard saddled his horse and rode as swiftly as the animal could gallop, but it was not fast enough to stop Blanfar's final act of revenge. When Alard arrived at the castle, Ligne's body had just been found drowned in a pool.

Alard ordered Blanfar bound and brought before him. In those days the owner of a castle had absolute power of life and death over his subjects. Alard sentenced Blanfar to be taken to the castle's inner courtyard and hacked by his axman into four quarters. He ordered the four quarters of flesh buried beneath stones in the four corners of the forest of St. Wandrille.

So the sentence was carried out. One would have thought that was the end of Blanfar, but stories of sightings of a most hideous ghost have passed down through the centuries.

On certain nights—nobody can predict when—the four masses of buried flesh are said to crawl out of their graves and come together to form the huge, bloody body of Blanfar. Her stinking ghost, sometimes carrying the body of her son, lumbers throughout the castle, trailing rotting flesh. Supposedly her desire to protect her son and her rage at Count Alard for killing him were too strong for her to remain buried. Her murderous energy continues to haunt the castle.

19

The Ghosts of Whaley House

They have been heard, seen, and even photographed—the ghosts of Whaley House in San Diego, California. The house has a long history of hauntings, but the earliest reported ghost did not even live there. He was hanged on the spot where the house was later built. It happened this way:

In 1852 a man named "Yankee Jim" Robinson was sentenced to die by hanging. He had been caught attempting to steal a pilot boat in San Diego harbor. The date for the execution was set and the hanging scaffold built. But the scaffold was too short. Instead of dropping fifteen feet and dying instantly of a broken neck, Yankee Jim dropped only five feet and died an agonizing death by strangulation that took about  fifteen minutes while he kicked and struggled at the end of the rope. Some say Yankee Jim was so angry about his prolonged suffering that he returned from the dead to haunt people for revenge.

SAN DIEGO, CALIFORNIA

Four years after Yankee Jim's execution, San Diego businessman Thomas Whaley began to build a house on the property where the hanging scaffold stood. In 1857 the house was completed and Whaley moved in with his new wife, Anna Eloise De Launay. The house was a showcase, and the Whaleys, who were socially prominent, gave many parties. But a restless, noisy spirit also inhabited the house.

The Whaley children heard heavy footsteps upstairs. The family believed that Yankee Jim's ghost, still angry over his painful death, haunted the house.

Lillian Whaley, the last of the six Whaley children, lived in the house until she died at the age of eighty-nine in 1953. After her death, the city planned to tear the house down, but a citizens' committee saved it and made it one of San Diego's historic homes.

Various psychics and mediums have visited the house. They say it is haunted by several ghosts, not just Yankee Jim. In 1964 a televised séance was held in Whaley House by talk-show host Regis Philbin, who invited famous ghost-hunter Dr. Hans Holzer and medium Sybil Leek to spend a night in the house. At 2:30 A.M. Philbin reported seeing an image of a woman float from the study, through the music room, and into the parlor.

Visitors to what is now called the Whaley House Museum have reported a variety of strange experiences. At least four ghosts are believed to dwell in the house: Anna and Thomas Whaley, Yankee Jim, and a girl named Washburn, who was a playmate of the Whaley children. Sometimes a phantom dog runs through the house, a baby cries, and a woman, believed to be Anna's spirit, sings. Cooking odors come from an empty kitchen, the odor of Thomas Whaley's favorite Havana cigars drifts from the main hall, and Anna's sweet-scented perfume is noticed all over the house.

As recently as 1992 a visitor took a photo with high-speed film that showed an unidentified woman. She is believed to be the ghost of a domestic worker hired by the Whaley children.

Whaley House Museum

Whaley House Museum opened in May 1960. According to director June Reading, visitors still report hearing footsteps and seeing ghosts. From time to time shadowy, unidentified figures appear in photographs.

If you dare, Whaley House Museum is open for tours daily from 10:00 A.M. to 4:30 P.M. Prices are $4.00 for adults, $3.00 for senior citizens, and $2.00 for juniors age 5–16. For more information contact: Whaley House Museum, 2482 San Diego Avenue, San Diego, CA 92110, or phone: 619-298-2482.

20

The Testifying Ghost

The seventeenth-century courtroom in Cornwall, England, was stifling hot, and the lawyers perspired heavily. It was a simple enough case: a moneylender was suing his debtor for repayment of a loan. But the debtor claimed he never borrowed any money. The case dragged on and on. Both the judge and the lawyers were eager to settle the matter.

"Your Lordship, there was a witness to this loan," the moneylender's lawyer suddenly announced.

"Then where is that witness?" the judge asked.

"That witness is Jan Tregeagle, who has gone to his grave," replied the debtor's lawyer. "He can hardly be called to testify."

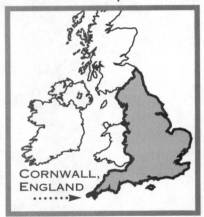

CORNWALL, ENGLAND ·······➤

There was a snicker from the spectators, but the judge looked stern and banged his gavel.

"If Tregeagle ever saw it, I wish to God he would come and declare it," the debtor exclaimed loudly.

Suddenly the door of the courtroom flew open and the filthy, foul-smelling ghost of Jan Tregeagle entered. No one spoke or breathed. Even the lawyers were speechless.

"He owes the sum," the ghost said, then walked to the debtor and whispered, "You will not find it easy to get rid of me."

Had the debtor known what lay in store, he would never have called on Tregeagle's ghost. He paid his debt, but from that moment forward, the debtor and the town of Cornwall were haunted by Tregeagle's ghost.

The ghost followed the debtor like a shadow, making noises in his bedroom, moving the curtains, beckoning him from the street. After many days and sleepless nights, the debtor was desperate to get rid of the ghost.

He went to the parish priest and begged for help. The priest performed an exorcism, which seemed to relieve the debtor of the ghost but did not banish the ghost from the town.

To get rid of Tregeagle's ghost, the priests came up with a plan that would keep the ghost busy for eternity.

Using exorcism rites, the priests sent the ghost to Dozmary Pool, believed to be a bottomless lake. They ordered him to empty the lake using a leaking limpet shell. But Tregeagle's ghost rebelled at such a job.

One night, during a terrible storm, Tregeagle ran away. Headless demon hounds chased him for miles. As the hounds pawed at his feet, the ghost's screams were heard for miles around.

Finally the priest drove away the hounds, and the noisy ghost was banished to Land's End at the tip of Cornwall, where few people lived. His new task was to carry sand from one cove around a high rocky headland to another cove. As before, the ghost howled whenever the wind and tides washed away his work.

Over the centuries the ghostly howlings seem to have disappeared; or, at least, people have stopped listening for them.

21

The Lonely Ghost of The Hermitage

On certain nights when the moon shines brightly, a beautiful young woman wearing a long white ball gown floats across the lawn of an old South Carolina plantation called The Hermitage. She enters the house and drifts upstairs to a room that was once hers. Frantically she opens drawers, looking for something that she will never find. Many people have seen her. They say she is the ghost of Alice Belin Flagg, a young woman who lived and died at The Hermitage.

MURRELLS INLET, SOUTH CAROLINA

Alice's older brother, Dr. Allard Belin Flagg, bought The Hermitage in 1848. He lived there with his widowed mother and his sister. He was known to be a kind and good doctor, but he always thought he knew what was best for everybody, including Alice.

Dr. Flagg decided that Alice should go to a fancy finishing school for girls in Charleston. This kind of education, he thought, would help her to meet and marry a wealthy, socially prominent man.

As love often goes its own way, Alice fell in love with a turpentine salesman. Dr. Flagg was furious and did everything he could to discourage the romance.

At the annual New Year's Saint Cecilia Ball, Alice's boyfriend gave her an engagement ring. She was overjoyed but knew better than to tell her brother, she wore the ring secretly on a ribbon around her neck.

Several months later she became ill with the dreaded fever of malaria, a tropical disease carried by mosquitoes. The headmistress of the school in Charleston sent a message to Dr. Flagg, and he left immediately with a servant to fetch Alice. He carried blankets in his carriage and tried to make Alice as comfortable as possible during the four-day journey back to The Hermitage. Unfortunately, by that time, Alice had become delirious.

As he examined her, Dr. Flagg discovered the ring. Angrily he tore it from her neck and threw it into a small creek alongside the house. Thinking she had lost her precious ring, Alice begged everyone who visited to help find it. Her ring was never found.

Each day she grew weaker and weaker. There were no antibiotics in the 1800s, and Dr. Flagg was helpless in treating her disease. Devastated by the loss of her ring, Alice died.

Dr. Flagg was as grief-stricken as anyone. He had his sister's corpse dressed in her white ball gown. She was buried temporarily on the grounds of The Hermitage until all the family members arrived weeks later for a proper funeral. Then her body was moved to the Flagg family lot in All Saints Cemetery.

But some people say that Alice never left The Hermitage. She still haunts the grounds and floats about the house searching for a ring she will never find.

22

The Ghost in the Library

Did you ever hear of a haunted library? The one in Bernardsville, New Jersey, has a resident ghost named Phyllis Parker.

Phyllis lived during the Revolutionary War. Her father owned Vealtown Tavern, a pub that is now the library's reading room. But long before it became part of Bernardsville Public Library, the Vealtown Tavern was like a small hotel. In addition to the bar and eating area, there were other rooms that were rented to tenants. One of the tenants was a Dr. Byram. He and Phyllis were attracted to each other, and they became lovers.

BERNARDSVILLE, NEW JERSEY

Unknown to Phyllis, Dr. Byram was a spy for the British. While he lived at the tavern he stole military plans from General Anthony Wayne, another guest and an officer with the American revolutionary army. Once Byram's mission was accomplished and he had the information, he disappeared. Phyllis was heartbroken. Byram didn't even say good-bye.

Byram was caught, convicted of spying for the enemy, and hanged. Then for some unknown reason his body was placed in a box and delivered to the tavern.

Phyllis was there when the large crate arrived. Not knowing what was inside, she opened it. When she saw her lover's body inside the box, she screamed and cried hysterically. The fact that he was a convicted spy didn't ease her anguish. She never got over the shock and had a mental breakdown.

Eventually the Vealtown Tavern closed, and the building was sold and converted to a home. No one thought anything more of Phyllis and Dr. Byram until 1877, a century later. In that year the owner of the house reported hearing a woman screaming. There were also other sounds—as if someone were opening and closing a box.

Another century passed. By then the old tavern had gone from being a home to one section of the Bernardsville Public Library. One day in 1977 a library clerk arrived early for her job. While she waited for someone to open the building, she saw a woman inside the library. Thinking it was her boss, the student was just about to get out of her car when her boss drove up beside her. They went inside the library and looked around. No one was there. Because of the stories about the strange occurrences in the old tavern, they felt that the figure must have been Phyllis's ghost.

Shortly thereafter a psychic brought one of her classes to the library. While there she felt vibrations that she believed were coming from the ghost of Phyllis. The psychic had a theory that the renovations to the building over the years had caused Phyllis's spirit to become active. Phyllis's ghost is believed to still haunt the Bernardsville Public Library, forever reliving that awful moment when she saw her lover cold in death.

57

23

The Phantom Ships of Goodwin Sands

Imagine you are on a ship during a storm. The wind roars. High waves rock the ship and sea spray wets the deck. Suddenly off the starboard bow a strange vessel floats into view—a ship with sails, the kind of ship that navigators sailed centuries ago. Where did it come from? What fool would try to sail such a vessel in a storm?

Suddenly the mysterious ship begins to sink. The captain on your ship sounds the alarm. "Lower the lifeboats!" But when the lifeboats reach the spot where the ship was last seen, there's nothing. No sign of a ship, no bodies, no floating wreckage. The ship was a phantom, a ghost ship.

One of the most haunted areas of the sea is Goodwin Sands, a dangerous sandbank that lies five miles off the coast of Deal in the British Isles, at the point where the English Channel flows into the North Sea. Over several centuries about 50,000 people have lost their lives in shipwrecks on the sandbank. The most famous phantom ship is a three-masted schooner named Lady Lovibond.

On February 13, 1748, Lady Lovibond ran aground on the sands and sank as it was bound for Oporto, Portugal. All aboard were drowned. From the beginning the voyage was considered unlucky, because the captain had brought his bride, Annetta, on board. In those days sailors were very superstitious and believed it was bad luck to take a woman to

Meeting the Lady?

The Lady Lovibond has appeared in 1798, 1848, 1898, and 1948. If the phantom ship keeps to its half-century schedule, it will be due again in 1998 and then in 2048.

If you're interested in seeing the ghost ship for yourself, save your money and plan a trip to Deal for the next scheduled sighting.

sea. But the real bad luck on this ship may have been the captain's first mate. According to legend, the first mate and the captain had been rivals for Annetta's love, but the captain won her as his wife. For revenge, the first mate murdered the helmsman and deliberately wrecked the ship.

No one will ever know whether the first mate or the sandbank was to blame for all the lost lives. But the spirits of those taken too soon from life return to reenact the terrible event.

Every 50 years, on February 13, the Lady Lovibond is seen running aground on Goodwin Sands. Its first appearance was in 1798; the crew on at least two ships reported seeing the phantom. The apparition looked so real that the captain of one of the ships, the Edenbridge, thought his own vessel was going to collide with it. He sent out lifeboats to rescue survivors, but no traces of a wrecked ship were found.

GOODWIN
SANDS,
OFF THE
COAST OF
ENGLAND

The Ghost of the Adelphi Theatre

In 1928 a comedic actress named June was putting on makeup in her dressing room at London's Adelphi Theatre. Already she could hear the audience taking their seats. Suddenly she felt something move across her arms, as if hands were holding her arms down to her sides. But no one else was in the room. She saw only her own face in the mirror.

Then her chaise lounge began to shake, and she saw a greenish light above her mirror. June was terrified. Was her mind playing tricks? Was she going crazy? Or was it the ghost of William Terriss, a nineteenth-century actor who had been murdered there . . . over thirty years ago?

Terriss's murder took place on December 16, 1897. Both Terriss and his girlfriend, actress Jessie Milward, were performing in a thriller called *Secret Service*. Also in the show was actor Richard Prince, who played a minor role. No one suspected that Prince was extremely jealous of Terriss and hated him. One day Prince bought a dagger with which to kill Terriss.

LONDON, ENGLAND

On the evening of the murder, Prince waited for Terriss to arrive at the stage door. As Terriss unlocked the door, Prince brutally stabbed him and left him to die. Jessie, Terriss's girlfriend, ran to his side. As Terriss lay dying in Jessie's arms, he whispered to her, "I'll be back."

Prince was convicted of murder and declared insane. He was sentenced to an institution for the criminally insane where he died in 1937 at the age of seventy-one.

Before Prince died, Terriss made good on his promise to return, at

least according to those who say they saw
his ghost. The first report came in
1928, thirty years after Terriss's
murder. A stranger who knew nothing
about the murder claimed he saw a man
dressed in gray Victorian clothes in
Maiden Lane, a street near the theater.
Suddenly the figure just disappeared.
From photographs he identified the ghost
as the murdered actor William Terriss.
That same year June had the scary experience in her dressing room.

Over the years many people believed they
saw Terriss's ghost. In 1956 it was reported
drifting around the Covent Garden
Underground Station, which is not far from
the theater. A spiritualist held a séance at
the station and produced a sketch of a man
who looked like Terriss.

The last reported sighting was in 1962
when night workmen reported seeing a
greenish light take the shape of a man and
float across the Adelphi Theatre's stage. It
then opened the stage curtains and moved into
the aisles, tipping the seats as it went.

William Terriss's ghost may still haunt the
Adelphi Theatre. In the grand tradition of the
stage, the show must go on; and for Terriss's
ghost, the show is not quite over.

The Ghost Clown of Jaipur

Prince Marwar, Maharaja of Jaipur, was absolute ruler of his two million subjects in the 1750s. He acted like a spoiled child, and spent most of the day lying on his couch at the royal palace in Amber, the capital of Jaipur. The prince ordered his ministers to entertain him if they wanted to keep their heads attached to their shoulders.

Prince Marwar was bored with everything and delighted only in the suffering of others. If a dancing girl missed a single step in her routine, he had her whipped. One evening he was so dissatisfied with his chief councillor's failure to provide entertainment that he had the man beheaded.

The ministers, who feared for their lives, heard about a French circus traveling from village to village. Hoping that might amuse the prince, they sent messengers to bring the circus to Amber.

For the next five years the circus performers and animals succeeded in entertaining Prince Marwar. His favorite performer was the circus clown, a young Spaniard named Pépé Dindoneau.

Never had the prince seen such a talent as Pépé. Not only could he perform all sorts of tricks, the slender, dark-haired young man walked a tightrope so cleverly that he seemed to dance on air.

The prince was so delighted by Pépé that he called for him at all hours of the day and night. Finally the prince dismissed the rest of the circus company. Pépé was the only entertainer he wanted.

When Pépé met a beautiful young woman named Arahna, they married and lived in the music pavilion, on the palace grounds.

For several years Pépé was able to make Prince Marwar laugh as no one else ever had. But finally a time came near the end of the 1750s when Prince Marwar no longer laughed at anything. He had become so fat that it took two large men to turn him in his bed, and he was almost blind. Soon the old prince died, and his brother, Prince Jai-Singh, became Maharaja.

By now Pépé and Arahna had three sons. Ten years passed, and then one night during the feast of the Hindu goddess Kali, Pépé was preparing to dance his old clown dance. Arahna and Nali, his oldest son, were standing nearby.

Suddenly a strange man who had been hiding in the shadows leapt out, waving a whip knotted with sharp metal points. The thug struck Arahna. Trying to protect Nali, Arahna grabbed the boy's hand and ran. In their haste, mother and son crashed into an old rotting wall that gave way, plunging both to their deaths on the rocks far below.

Pépé and several others grabbed the thug and strangled him with his own whip. They made their way down the steep ravine and found Arahna and Nali crushed to death in a rocky crevice. Pépé decided to leave the bodies. He and his friends piled up stones to seal their rocky grave.

For days Pépé could not eat or speak. Still wearing his clown costume, he walked the empty corridors of the palace. Then he disappeared for several months. When he returned, ragged and dirty, he never did his clown act again. He died a broken-hearted old man, but people say his ghost still returns after more than two centuries of haunting.

Sometimes he appears as a colorfully costumed young clown turning cartwheels and seeming to walk on air. On other nights when the moon is full, an old clown wearing a frayed costume peers over a wall near the crumbling, abandoned palace. He always seems to be looking for something. Sometimes he is seen in the ravine, poking among the rocks. At dawn he returns to the palace, haunting the place where he gave so much joy and found such sorrow.